Basic Truths Series 4-6

by
Bambi Betts

Illustrated by
Brittany Betts

GR

GEORGE RONALD

OXFORD

George Ronald, Publisher
Oxford
www.grbooks.com

This edition 2008

Originally published in 1989 as three separate books:
0-85398-284-8 What's Fair ...
0-85398-283-X When Nothing Goes Right
0-85398-285-6 When I Pray

A catalogue record for this book is available
from the British Library

ISBN 978-0-85398-526-6

4

What's Fair . . .

If you use your crayons to make a beautiful
picture on a piece of paper . . .

everyone is happy. You are happy because you worked hard and made something beautiful.

Your mother and father are happy because you
tried hard. They give you a kiss or a hug and say
'What a lovely drawing!'

But . . . if you used your crayons to make a
beautiful picture on your bedroom wall . . .

everyone is UNhappy. You are unhappy because
you really do know that bedroom walls are not
for drawing on.

Your mother and father are unhappy because
the wall has crayon on it and THEY know that YOU
know all about bedroom walls and crayons.

They may take your crayons away for a day and say, 'Please don't do this again.'
That is what we call justice.

Bahá'u'lláh teaches us that justice is a very
important thing to have now in the world.
It means that people should be treated fairly.
When someone does something nice or good,
or in a way that is helpful . . .

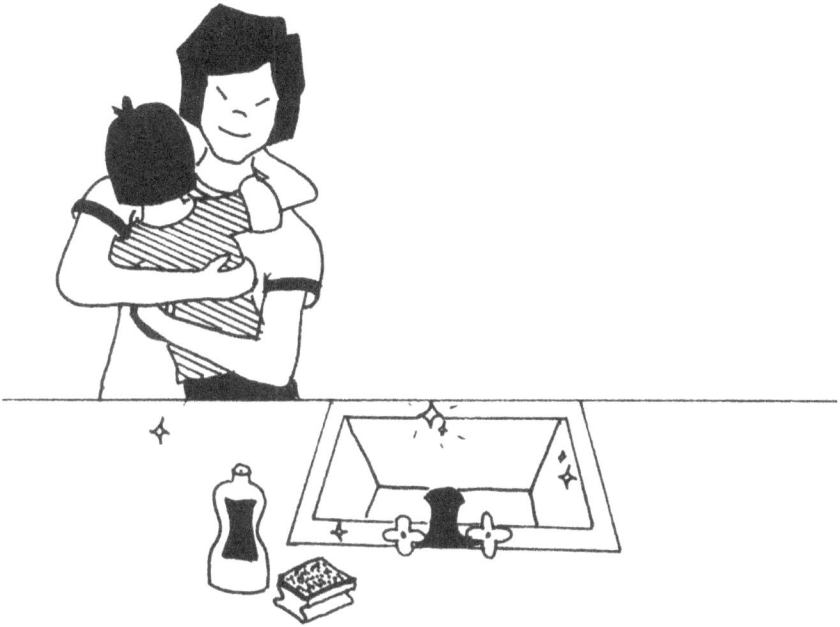

then he should be rewarded. That means he should be told and shown that he did a good thing, just like you get a special hug or kiss or maybe even a special treat when you do something well.

When someone does something he really shouldn't do then he should be punished.

That means he should be told or shown that he did something that was not right, just like you may have your crayons taken away if you draw on the wall.

If we only got rewards then we might go on thinking that it was all right to go on writing on walls . . .

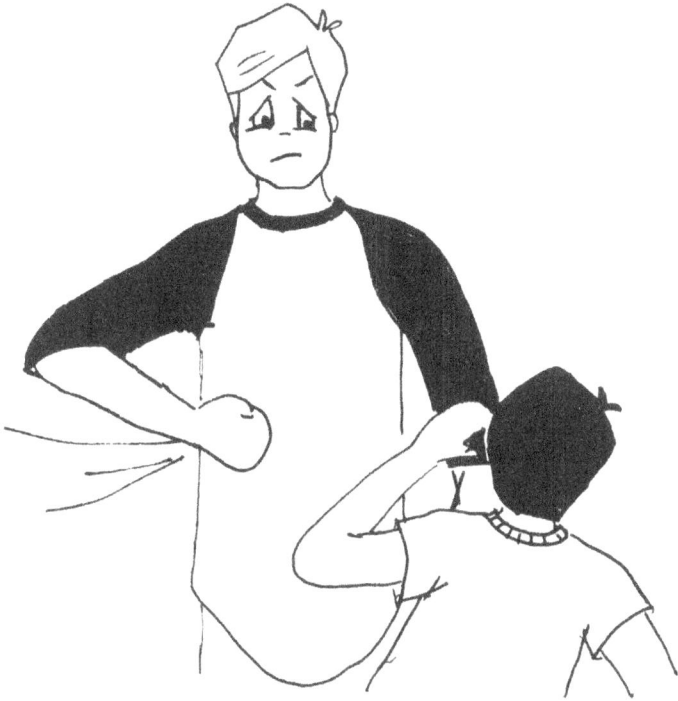

Or hurting other people . . .
or other not-so-good things.

And if we only ever got punished then we just
might never learn the good ways of doing things.
Or we might feel that no one cared,
so why even try?

Both of these are ways of helping people learn
more about how to behave and to make the
world a nicer place to live in.

That is why Bahá'u'lláh says to have justice
(remember, that means fairness) we need to
have rewards AND punishment.

Now that sounds pretty fair to me.
How about you?

5

When Nothing
Goes Right

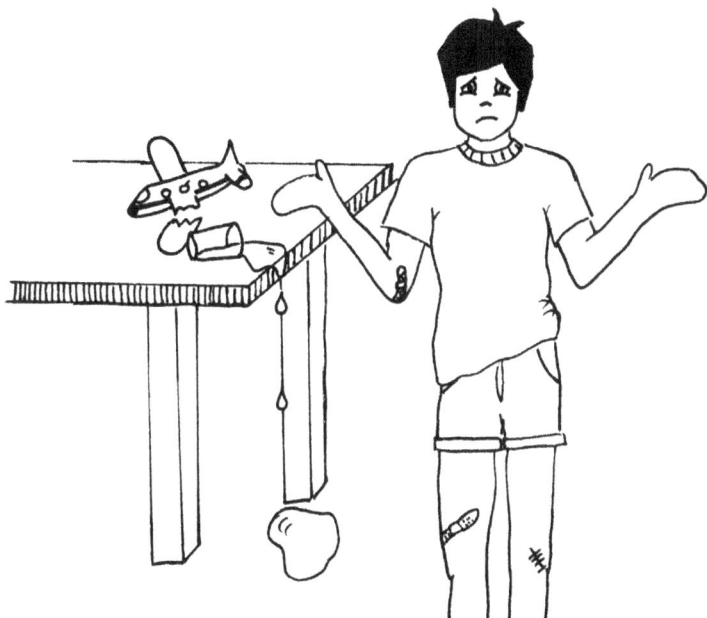

There are times when nothing seems to go right.

You've waited all morning to visit the park . . .

then your mother says she's sorry, but she won't
be able to take you at all today.

You've invited all your friends over for a party ...

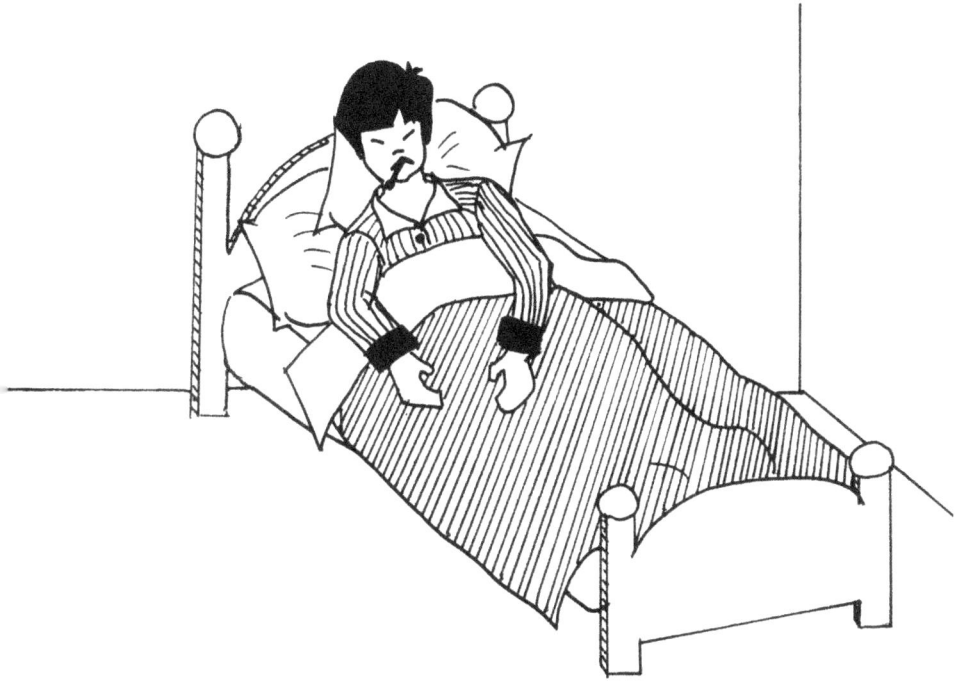

and then you get sick and they can't come.

you've worked very hard on a special drawing . . .

and it accidentally gets thrown away.

Everyone has these things happen to them. And it can feel terrible ... and so unfair.

But do you know what? Bahá'u'lláh tells us that these things that happen to us are really ...

GIFTS! Now that must sound strange. But Bahá'u'lláh says it's true. Oh, they're not the kind of gifts that come wrapped up in boxes, like you might give to someone you love because you want to make them happy. These troubles are gifts that God gives us to help our souls grow.

If you need to learn to have patience, God gives you a chance to learn by giving you times to wait.

If you need to learn to share, God gives you a chance to learn by giving you times to share.

If you need to learn to be helpful, God gives you a chance to learn by giving you times to be helpful.

These troubles really are gifts because they are given to us by God, who loves us, to make us better and stronger and happier. Bahá'u'lláh even says that sometimes in our prayers we should ask God for more chances – more tests and difficulties – to make us stronger. Imagine that!

So the next time you have to wait for your lunch
and you're so hungry . . .

or your mother says she can't read to you right
now even though you've been waiting
ALL afternoon . . .

you can try to smile and ask yourself,
'Is this a gift from God to make me strong?'

6

When I Pray

Every day, often many times a day, you eat food – fruit or vegetables or bread or meat or other things.

That food is what makes your body keep going . . .

and growing.

What would happen if you stopped eating for a
day ... or two ... or three ... or four?

The longer you went without food, the weaker you would become. Your body cannot live without food.

Did you know there is another part of you that
needs to be fed too? You can't see it like you can
see your body, but we know it's there because
God has told us that it is. It is your soul. It's part
of you that lives on and on . . . forever.
It's what makes you really you.

Just as your body can't grow without food, your
soul can't grow properly without prayer.

Your soul needs prayer every day to keep it healthy and growing. It is fed by remembering God.

Prayer is one way of remembering God ... of making a connection with Him ... of talking to Him ... thanking Him ... and asking Him to help us be strong.

And God really does hear your prayers!
Sometimes it's hard to imagine that, especially
since you can't hear God or see Him. But
Bahá'u'lláh promises that prayers are heard and
answered ...

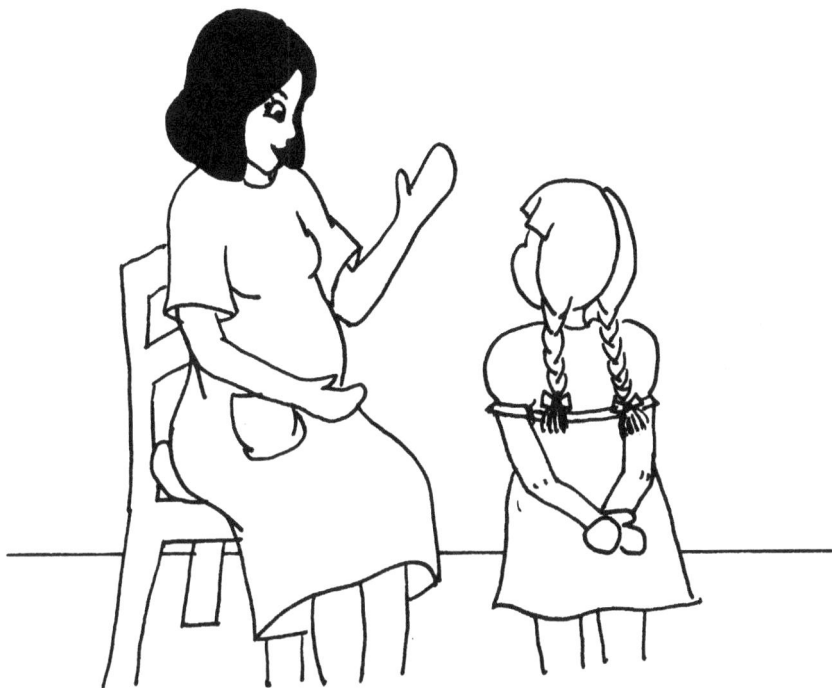

even though sometimes it takes a long time for
us to notice the answer . . .

and other times the answer is very different
from what we thought it would be.

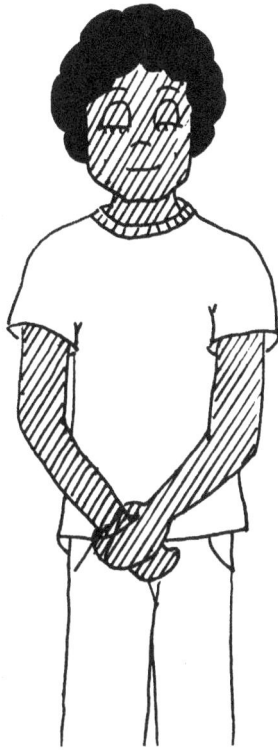

People pray in many different ways.
Some close their eyes . . .

some look up or down . . .

some fold their arms . . . some say the words
loudly, some say them softly.

All are trying, in their own way, to become closer to God ... to let God know they need His help and that they love Him and that their souls need to be fed with prayer.

How do you pray?

Can you remember to keep your soul strong
and growing? The Báb, Bahá'u'lláh and
'Abdu'l-Bahá have written many prayers to help
us. Here is one you can start with:

O Lord! Plant this tender seedling in the garden
of Thy manifold bounties, water it from the
fountains of Thy loving-kindness and grant that
it may grow into a goodly plant through the
outpourings of Thy favour and grace.
Thou art the Mighty and the Powerful.

'Abdu'l-Bahá

'From the very beginning, the children must receive divine education and must continually be reminded to remember their God.'
'Abdu'l-Bahá

Guidelines for Parents
by Bambi Betts

One morning, my three children and I were sitting on the bedroom floor, playing together. We had just returned home the night before from a Bahá'í conference. Quite suddenly, the four-year-old said, 'At the conference they told us that mankind is one.'

'That's true,' she continued, 'if mankind is one, then when will it be two?' Many parents have experienced the sweetness and humour of such misperceptions in their young children. They enrich the family culture and become endearing tales for the grandchildren. However, as parents we have the awesome responsibility to transmit to our children the basic truths concerning existence. It is all too easy to read a story or give a short lesson to a child and assume that because we understand the message (i.e. mankind is one), that the child does as well. If mankind is to progress toward the creation of a better civilization, and individuals toward the refinement of spiritual qualities, this responsibility cannot be left to chance. Like all other aspects of development, it requires care and attention consistent with the needs, capacities and perceptions of each particular phase of development.

The Báb assures us that even the youngest of children today will be wiser than the wisest man of past generations. Again, this will not happen by chance. The Basic Truths Series is designed to assist you in providing the basic vocabulary and concepts needed to begin the process of ensuring that the words become firm concepts, consistent with reality as well as relevant to your child's current perception of life. Obviously, none of the books is intended to be a thorough discussion of the topic, rather a gentle introduction to the world of concepts from the viewpoint of a young child.

Most parents will know their own child well enough to make the best use of these books. However, so that each of you does not feel he must re-invent the wheel, a few ideas from other parents might prove useful.

1. Follow the child's lead. Let him stop you and ask questions or make comments. Simply by listening you will pick up valuable clues about his level of understanding.
2. The illustrations are an integral part of learning for young children. Use them to bring the concept closer to the child's own experience.
3. Whenever possible, use examples from the child's daily life to make a point come alive.
4. Remind the child often that these ideas came from Bahá'u'lláh.
5. Ask the child to tell you about the book after you've read it. A young child will typically focus on one illustration or one part which is close to his own experience. This is another useful tool for determining the level of his comprehension.